Crash Course in French.

The Quickest Way to Learn Essential French

BookCaps™ Study Guides

www.bookcaps.com

Table of Contents

Introduction: Do you speak French?

Parlais Vous Française? {pahrleh voo frahnseh}

Bonjour! Congratulations for making the first step on a journey to learn French, a language that constitutes enormous part of world's cultural heritage, a language of beauty, literature, art and science, a language that no sophisticated spirit can resist.

French is an official language (or one of the official languages) in France, Luxemburg, Belgium, Switzerland, Monaco, Canada and many African countries. It has served as a main diplomatic tongue for international communication for past two hundred years and is still used as one of the official United Nations languages. Rough estimates indicate that around 300 million people in 50 countries all over the world use French! Imagine being able to freely communicate with them, opening yourself up for a myriad of new personal, business and cultural opportunities.

The purpose of this handbook is to help you on that journey by introducing you to the basics of French language, without encroaching too much on the complex fields of grammar. You will learn simple words and dialogs that represent you, corresponding to a foreigner in a French speaking country. But, while memorizing these dialogs, you will also learn grammar, without even realizing it. The patterns of French grammar will make an imprint in your mind on a subconscious level, making you able to easily replace old words with new ones and construct completely new sentences!

Pronunciation

la prononciation {lah prohn-ohn-seeya-seeyohn}

French belongs to the group of very difficult and complex languages when it comes to pronunciation. There are many intricacies you will need to pay heed to, such as multiple sounds for one single letter, silent letters and countless exceptions to all of the rules. Our goal is to simplify the learning process for the beginners and help you to get started. The pronunciation rules listed here will be enough for you to learn how to pronounce majority of the words you come across. However, once you are ready to expand your knowledge of the French language, you will need to learn more examples and exceptions.

Vowels

Letter	Pronunciation	Explanation	Example
è ê	eh	Opened "e" as in 'cat' Position your mouth like you want to pronounce "ah" but pronounce "eh" instead	frère {frehr} – brother fête {feht} - holiday
é	ay	Closed "e" as in 'dazed' Position your mouth like you want to pronounce "ee", but pronounce "eh" instead.	vérité {vehreetay} - truth
e		Voiceless "e" as in 'the'	Mercredi {mehrkr¢dee} – Wednesday
e		Silent "e" as in 'fore'	appeler {applay} – to call
i	ee y	in front of the consonant – as in 'kit' in front of the vowel – as in 'yet'	vite{vit} – fast cahier {kahyay} - notebook

u	uu	As in '*lune*'. Position your mouth like you want to pronounce "oo", but pronounce "ee" instead.	mur {muuhr} - wall
y	ee y	when alone or next to a consonant, as in 'Nancy' between vowels as in '*paying*'	lyre {leer} – lyre Maya {Mah-yah}- name Maya
ai **ei**	eh	It is usually opened, as in '*set*'	français {frahnseh} - French seize {sehz} - sixteen
au **eau**	oh	closed, as in '*bone*'	Paul {Pohl} - name Paul l'eau {loh} - water
eu **oeu** **ue**	euh	Position your mouth like you want to pronounce "oh", but pronounce "eh" instead.	deux {duh} - two soeur {suhr} - sister cueillir {kuhyeer } - to pick
oi	wah	as in '*Croatia*'	trois {trwa} - three

Nasal Vowels

Letter	Pronunciation	Explanation	Example
an, am **en, em**	ahn	As in '*bank*'	restaurant {restorahn} - restaurant chambre {shahnbreh} - room cent {sahn} - hundred
in, im **ain, aim** **ein, eim** **yn, ym**	ehn	As in '*men*'	cinq {sehnk} -five faim {fehn} - hunger plein {plehn} - full sympathique {sehnpahtick}
on, om	ohn	As in '*bonbon*'	bon {bohn} - good nom {nohn} - name
un, um	uuhn	As in '*parfume*'	une {uuhn} - one

Consonants

Letter	Pronunciation	Explanation	Example
c	s k	in front of *e, i, y*, as in '*ice*' in front of *a, o, u* and next to consonants, as in '*car*'	facile {fassill} - easy car {kahr} - because
cc	x	in front of *e* and *i* as in '*Xena*'	accent {axahn} - accent
ch	sh k	in front of a vowel, as in '*share*' in front of a consonant '*Chris*'	chapeau {shappoh} - hat chronique {krohnick} - chronic
g	zh g	in front of e, i, y, as in '*mirage*' in front of a, o, u and next to consonants, as in '*go*'	gilet {zhileh} - razor grand {grahn} - big
ge	zh	as in '*giraffe*'	Georges {zhohrzh} - name George
gu	g	in front of a vowel, as in '*gepard*'	guerre {gehr} - war
gue	g	at the end of word, as in '*ding*'	langue {lahng} - language

gn	ny	as in 'onion'	gagner {gahnyeh} - win
il, ill	eel	at the beginning of a word, as in 'pillar'	illusion {illuseeohn} - illusion
	eey	behind a consonant	famille {fameey} - family
	y	behind a vowel, as in 'Murrey'	soleil {sohley} - sun
j	zh		jeunes {zhuhn} - young
ph	f	as in 'philosophy'	éléphant {elefahn}
q, qu	k	as in 'quote'	cinq {sahnk} - five
s	s	at the beginning of a word and next to consonants, as in 'sun'	escalier {eskaleeyeh} - stairs
	z	between vowels, as in 'easy'	maison {mezohn} - house
ss	s	as in 'passage'	passer {pahseh} - to pass
x	gz	as in 'example'	exemple {egzehnple} - example
	z		deuxième {douzyehm} - second
	s		six {sees} - six
	ks		expliquer {eksplikeh} - to explain

Pronunciation Tips

1. Letter 'e' is never pronounced if placed at the end of a word - *il chante {il shahnt} - he sings*
2. Letter 'h' is never pronounced. *homme {ohm} - man*
3. Consonants: **x**, **p**, **s**, **t**, **d**, **g** and **z**, are almost never pronounced when found at the end of a word.

deux {duh} - two
trois {trwa} - three
beaucoup {bokoo} - plenty
salut {salew} -hi   grand {grahn} - big
long {lohn} - long
assez {asseh} – enough

4.   Consonants: **r**, **l**, **f** and **c** are almost always pronounced if found at the end of a word.

soir {swar} - evening
hotel {otel} - hotel neuf {nuhf} - nine
avec {avek} - with

Numbers

Les numéros {le numeroh}

1-10

One - Un {ahn}

Two - Deux {duh}

Three - Trois {trwa}

Four - Quatre {katr}

Five - Cinq {sahnk}

Six - Six {sees}

Seven - Sept {set}

Eight - Huit {weet}

Nine - Neuf {nuhf}

Ten -   Dix {dees}

11- 20

Eleven -   onze {ohnz}

Twelve - douze {dooz}

Thirteen - treize {trehz}

Fourteen - quatorze {kahthorz}

Fifteen - quinze {kanz}

Sixteen - seize {sehz}

Seventeen - dix-sept {deeset}

Eighteen - dix-huit {deezweet}

Nineteen - dix-neuf {deeznuhf}

Twenty - vingt {vahn}

21-20

Twenty one- vingt et un{vahntehahn}

Twenty two - vingt-deux{vahntduh}

Twenty three - vingt-trois{vahntrwa}

Twenty four - vingt-quatre{vahntkatr}

Twenty five - vingt -cinq {vahntsahnk}

Twenty six - vingt-six{vahntsees}

Twenty seven - twenty eight -vingt-sept {vahntset}

Twenty nine - vingt-huit {vahntweet}

Thirty -vingt-neuf trente{vahntnuhf trahnt}

31-40

Thirty one - trente et un {trahntehahn}

Thirty Two - trente-deux {trahntduh}

Thirty Three - trente-trois {trahntrwa}

Thirty four - trente-quatre {trahntkatr}

Thirty five - trente-cinq {trahntsahnk}

Thirty six - trente-six {trahntsees}

Thirty seven - trente-sept {trahntset}

Thirty eight - trente-huit {trahntweet}

Thirty nine - trente-neuf {trahntnuhf}

Forty - quarante {kahrahnt}

41-50

Forty one- quarante et un {kahrahntehahn}

Forty two - quarante-deux {kahrahntduh}

Forty three - quarante-trois {kahrahntrwa}

Forty four- quarante-quatre {kahrahntkatr}

Forty five - quarante-cinq {kahrahntsahnk}

Forty six - quarante-six {kahrahntsees}

Forty seven - quarante-sept {kahrahntset}

Forty eight - quarante-huit {kahrahntweet}

Forty nine - quarante-neuf {kahrahntnuhf}

Fifty - cinquante {sahnkahnt}

51-60

Fifty one - cinquante et un {sahnkahntehahn}

Fifty two - cinquante-deux {sahnkahntduh}

Fifty three - cinquante-trois {sahnkahntrwa}

Fifty four - cinquante-quatre {sahnkahntkatr}

Fifty five - cinquante-cinq {sahnkahntsahnk}

Fifty six - cinquante-six {sahnkahntsees}

Fifty seven - cinquante-sept {sahnkahntset}

Fifty eight - cinquante-huit {sahnkahntweet}

Fifty nine - cinquante-neuf {sahnkahntnuhf}

Sixty - soixante {soahsahnt}

61-70

sixty one -soixante et un {soahsahntehahn}

sixty two - soixante-deux {soahsahntduh}

sixty three- soixante-trois {soahsahnttrwa}

sixty four - soixante-quatre {soahsahntkatr}

sixty five -soixante-cinq {soahsahntsahnk}

sixty six -soixante-six {soahsahntsees}

sixty seven - soixante-sept {soahsahntset}

sixty eight - soixante-huit {soahsahntweet}

sixty nine - soixante-neuf {soahsahntnuhf}

seventy - soixante-dix {soahsahntdees}

71-80

Seventy one - soixante et onze {soahsahntehohnz}

Seventy two - soixante-douze {soahsahntdooz}

Seventy three - soixante-treize {soahsahntrehz}

Seventy four - soixante-quatorze {soahsahntkahthorz}

Seventy five - soixante-quinze {soahsahntkanz}

Seventy six - soixante-seizev{soahsahntsehz}

Seventy seven - soixante-dix-sept {soahsahntdeeset}

Seventy eight - soixante-dix-huit {soahsahntdeezweet}

Seventy nine - soixante-dix-neuf {soahsahntdeeznuhf}

Eighty - quatre-vingts {katrvahn}

81-90

Eighty one - quatre-vinght-un {katrvahntahn}

Eighty two - quatre-vingt-deux {katrvahnduh}

Eighty three - quatre-vingt-trois {katrvahntrwa}

Eighty four - quatre-vingt-quatre {katrvahnkatr}

Eighty five - quatre-vingt-cinq {katrvahnsahnk}

Eighty six - quatre-vingt-six {katrvahnsees}

Eighty seven - quatre-vingt-sept {katrvahnset}

Eighty eight - quatre-vingt-huit {katrvahntweet}

Eighty nine - quatre-vingt-neuf {katrvahnuhf}

Ninety - quatre-vingt-dix - {katrvahndees}

91-100

Ninety one - quatre-vingt-onze {katrvahntohnz}

Ninety two - quatre-vingt-douze {katrvahndooz}

Ninety three - quatre-vingt-treize {katrvahntrehz}

Ninety four - quatre-vingt-quatorze {katrvahnkahthorz}

Ninety five - quatre-vingt-quinze {katrvahnkanz}

Ninety six -quatre-vingt-seize   {katrvahnsehz}

Ninety seven - quatre-vingt-dix-sept {katrvahndeeset}

Ninety eight - quatre-vingt-dix-huit {katrvahndeezweet}

Ninety nine - quatre-vingt-dix-neuf {katrvahndeeznuhf}

Days of the Week

Les Jours de la semaine {leh zhoor d¢ la s¢mahn}

Monday
lundi *{lundee}*

Tuesday
mardi *{mahrdee}*

Wednesday
mercredi *{mehrkr¢dee}*

Thursday
jeudi *{zheuhdee}*

Friday
vendredi *{vahndrdee}*

Saturday
samedi *{sahmdi}*

Sunday
dimanche *{deemahnsh}*

There is no capitalization of days and months in French language.

Months and Seasons

Les mois et les saisons

January

janviere {zhahnvyay}

February

février {fayvreeyay}

March

march {mahrs}

April

avril {ahvreel}

May

mai {meh}

June

juin {zhwan}

July

juillet *{zhweeyeh}*

Avgust
août *{oot}*

September

septembre *{sehptahnbr}*

October

octobre *{ohktohbr}*

November

novembre *{nohvahnbr}*

December

décembre *{daysahnbr}*

Spring
le printemps *{lé prehntahn}*

Summer
l'été *{laytay}*

Fall
l'automne *{lohtohn}*

Winter
l'hiver *{leevehr}*

Colors

Les coulors {lay koolewhr}

Yellow

jaune *{zhon}*

Green

vert *{ vehr}*

Black

noir *{nwahr}*

White

blanc *{blahn}*

Grey
gris *{gree}*

Blue
bleu *{bluh}*

Violet
violet *{violet}*

Purple
mauve *{mov}*

Red

rouge *{roozh}*

Orange
orange *{ohrahnzh}*

Navy

bleu marin *{bluh marehn}*

Pink
rose *{rohz}*

Family

La famille {lah fahmeey}

Mother
la mère *{lah mehr}*

Father
le père *{lé pehr}*

Brother
le frère *{lé frehr}*

Sister
la soeur *{lah seuhr}*

Cousin
la cousine (f) / **le cousin** (m) *{lah koozin/lé koozahn}*

Grandma
la grand-mère *{lah grahnmehr}*

Grandpa
le grand-père *{lé grahnpehr}*

Aunt
la tante *{lah tahnt}*

Uncle
l'oncle *{lohnkl}*

Nephew
le neveu *{lé néveuh}*

Niece
la nièce *{lah nyehs}*

The Body

Le Corps {lə corp}

Phrases

head

la tête {lah teht}

face

le visage {lǿ veesahzh}

eyes

les yeux {lez yew}

eyebrow

la sourcil {lah soorseel}

nose

le nez {lǿ neh}

lips

les lèvres {leh lehvr}

mouth

la bouche {lah boosh}

tooth

la dent {lah dahn}

tongue

la langue {lah lahng}

chin

le menton {lȼ mahntohn}

cheek

la joue {la zhoo}

ear

l'oreill {lohrey}

hair

les cheveux {leh shȼveu}

neck

le cou {lȼ koo}

shoulder

l'épaule {lehpohl}

Body-related Phrases

Expressions liés au corps

My head hurts.
J'ai mal à la tête

I cut my finger.
J'ai coupé mon doigt

I wash my teeth every day.
Je me lave les dents tous les jours.

My hair is long and black.
Mes cheveux sont longs et noirs.

You have beautiful eyes.
Vous avez de beaux yeux.

I twisted my ankle.
Je me suis déboîté la cheville.

My nails are too long, I have to cut them.
Mes ongles sont trop longs, je dois les couper.

My shoulders are so tense.
Mes épaules sont tellement tendues.

I wash my hands with soap.
Je me lave les mains avec du savon.

She has beautiful legs.
Elle a de belles jambes.

Clothes

Vêtements {vetmahn}

Phrases

shirt
la chemise *{lah shemeez}*

t-shirt
le t-shirt *{lé tee shęrt}*

blouse

la blouse *{lah blooz}*

sweater

le pull *{lé pewl}*

jacket

la veste *{lah vehst}*

coat
le manteau *{lé mahntoh}*

suit
le costume *{lé kohstuum}*

dress
la robe *{lah rohb}*

skirt
la jupe *{lah zhoop}*

pants
le pantalon *{lé pahntahl-ohn}*

tracksuit
le survêtement *{lé suurvehtmahn}*

bra
le soutien-gorge *{lé soothyahn gorzh}*

panties

le slip *{lé slip}*

underwear
le caleçon *{lé kahlsohn}*

nightgown
la chemise de nuit *{lah shemeez dé nui}*

socks
la chaussette *{lah shohset}*

gloves
les gants *{leh gahn}*

shoe
la chaussure *{lah shohsewr}*

sneakers

les chaussures de sport *{leh shosyr dé spor}*

tie
la cravate *{lah krahvaht}*

hat
le chapeau *{lé shahpoh}*

belt
la ceinture *{lah sahntuur}*

shawl
le châle *{lé shahl}*

purse
le sac à main *{lé sahk-ah-mahn}*

umbrella
le parapluie *{lé pahrahplwee}*

watch

la montre *{lah mohntr}*

earring
boucle d'oreille *{booklé dohrey}*

necklace
le collier *{lé kohleeyeh}*

bracelet
le bracelet *{lé brasleh}*

ring
la bague *{lah bahg}*

Clothes-related phrases

Expressions liées aux vêtements

What a beautiful dress!
Quelle jolie robe!

I saw a lovely necklace in a jewelry store.
J'ai vu un joli collier dans une bijouterie.

I have a nightgown that is made from cotton.
J'ai une chemise de nuit en coton.

You will need a warm sweater this winter.
Vous aurez besoin d'un pull chaud cet hiver.

She has the same hat as I.
Elle a le même chapeau comme moi.

Your shoes look very comfortable.
Vos chaussures ont l'air très confortable.

How much does this belt cost?
Combien coûte cette ceinture?

I need an ironed shirt for tomorrow.
J'ai besoin d'une chemise repassée pour demain.

He looks very elegant in that suit.
Il est très élégant dans ce costume.

I love the color of that jacket!
J'aime la couleur de cette veste!

Direction

La Direction {lah deereksyohn}

Phrases

right
à droite *{ah drwat}*

left

à gauche *{ah gosh}*

up
en haut *{ahn oh}*

down
en bas *{ahn bah}*

straight ahead
tout droite *{too drwat}*

behind
derrière *{dehryehr}*

in front of
devant *{dehvahn}*

next to
à côté *{ah kohteh}*

north

le nord *{lé nohr}*

south
le sud *{lé suud}*

east

l'est *{lehst}*

west

l'ouest *{lwest}*

north-east
le nord-est *{lé nohrdehst}*

north-west
le nord-ouest *{lé nohrdwest}*

south-east
le sud-est *{lé suudest}*

south-west
le sud-ouest *{lé sydwest}*

near
près de *{preh dé}*

close
proche *{prosh}*

far
loin *{lwan}*

inside
à l'intérieur *{ah-lahntereeyewr}*

outside
dehors *{deohr}*

over

sur *{suur}*

under
au-dessus de *{odehsu dé}*

crossroad
l'intersection *{ahntérseksyohn}*

corner
le coin *{lé kwahn}*

street
la rue *{lah ruu}*

block
le quartier *{lé kartyey}*

to show
montrer *{montreh}*

where
ou *{oo}*

to reach
arriver *{areeveh}*

Direction-related Phrases

Excuse me, where is the pharmacy?
Excusez-moi, où est la pharmacie?

Pharmacy is straight ahead, behind the corner.
La pharmacie est tout droite, derrière le coin.

The bus station is very near
Arrêt de bus est très près d'ici.

Zoo is on the other side of the park.
Zoo est de l'autre côté du parc.

Follow the main road to the north.
Suivez la route principale vers le nord.

Take a walk to the downtown.
Aller à pied jusqu'au centre-ville.

City gates are on the west.
Portes de la ville sont a l'ouest.

In front of the hotel, there is one small cafe.
Devant l'hôtel il y a un petit café.

My child is waiting for me in front of the building.
Mon enfant m'attend devant le bâtiment.

I take a bus in front of my house.
Je prends l'autobus devant la maison.

Where does the boat leave from?
D'où part le bateau?

How can I reach the other side?
Comment puis-je arriver sur l'autre côté?

What is there on the island?
Qu'y-a-t'-il sur l'île?

My cousin lives close to the cathedral.
Mon cousin habite près de la cathédrale.

Could you please tell me where the park is?
Pourriez-vous me dire où se trouve le parc?

This crossroad looks familiar, doesn't it?
Ce croisement semble familier, n'est-ce pas?

Is the hotel far from here?
L'hôtel, c'est loin d'ici ?

That store is near the bus station.
Ce magasin est situé près de l'arrêt de bus.

Please come inside, it is cold.
Entrez à l'intérieur je vous en pris, il fait froid.

She is waiting for him outside.
Elle l'attend dehors.

I saw a lovely coffee-shop next to your house.
J'ai vu un joli café à côté de votre maison.

Does this bus go to the downtown?
Est ce que cet bus vas jusqu'au centre?

To reach the downtown, turn right.
Pour aller au centre-ville, tourner à droite.

What is the name of this street?
Quel est le nom de cette rue?

I would like to climb to the top of this hill.
J'aimerais bien me monter au sommet de cette colline.

Where should I go from here?
Où dois-je aller d'ici?

How can I find the police station?
Comment puis-je trouver le commissariat?

How far is the nearest train station?
A quelle distance se trouve la gare la plus proche?

Is the river bank close to the center?
La rivière, c'est près du centre-ville?

Should I go left or right?
Il faut que je m'en aille à gauche ou à droite?

Shopping
Courses *{koors}*

Phrases

shopping mall
le centre commercial *{lé sahntr kohmerseeyell}*

groceries
produits alimentaires *{prodwee ahleemehntehr}*

to buy
acheter *{ahshteh}*

to pay
payer *{pehyeh}*

to wrap
envelopper *{ahnvloppeh}*

to return
retourner *{rhtoorneh}*

to try out

essayer *{eessayay}*

expensive
cher *{shehr}*

cheap
pas cher *{pah shehr}*

color
la couleur *{lah koolewhr}*

quality
la qualité *{lah kahleetay}*

sample
échantillon *{ehshahnteeyohn}*

present

cadeau *{kahdoh}*

books

livres *{leevr}*

bakery
boulangerie *{boolahnzhree}*

counter

caisse *{kehs}*

shopping card

panier d'achat *{pahnyeh dashah}*

bag
sac *{sak}*

fresh food
produits frais *{prodwee freh}*

cosmetic products
produits cosmétiques *{prodwee kosmehteek}*

discount

prix réduit *{pree redwee}*

special offer
offre spéciale *{ophr spehseeyal}*

furniture

meubles *{mewbl}*

accessories
accessoires *{aseswahr}*

jewelry

bijouterie {beezhootree}

antiques

les antiquités {lehz ahnteekeetay}

butcher
le boucher *{lé booshay}*

patisserie
la pâtisserie *{lah pahteesree}*

dairy products
produits laitiers *{prodwee lehtyeh}*

flower shop
le fleuriste *{l¢ flureest}*

newspaper
la presse *{lah prehs}*

dry cleaner
nettoyage à sec {nehtoyazh ahsehk}

seller
le vendeur {l¢ vahnduhr}

toys
les jouets *{leh zhweh}*

hardware
la quincaillerie *{kahnkayree}*

watch maker
la horlogerie *{ohrlohrzhree}*

photographer
photographe *{photograph}*

stationary
papeterie *{pahpehtree}*

household equipment
articles ménagers *{arteekl mehnahzhe}*

sports equipment

articles de sport *{arteekl dé spohr}*

office equipment
articles de bureau {arteekl dé byroh}

school equipment
articles scolaire *{arteekl skoolehr}*

pharmacy
pharmacie *{pharmahsee}*

beauty salon
salon de beauté *{salohn dé bohtay}*

market
marché *{mahrshay}*

make up
maquillage *{makeeyahzh}*

utensils
ustensiles *{ystahnseel}*

automotive equipment
équipements automobiles *{ekeepmahn otomobeel}*

appliances

appareils *{apahrey}*

supplies
provisions *{proveezyohn}*

Shopping-related phrases

Expressions liées aux achats

How much does it cost?
Combien ça coûte?

Please give me one bottle of milk.
Donnez-moi une bouteille de lait, s'il vous plaît.

Do you have fresh bread?
Avez-vous du pain frais?

Please give me one more slice?
Donnez-moi encore une tranche, s'il vous plait.

I would like to try it out.
Je voudrais l'essayer

Excuse me, where is the fresh food department?
Excusez-moi, où est le rayon frais?

I am looking for low priced items.
Je cherche des articles à prix bas

Let's go to the shopping mall!
Allons-y au centre commercial!

I am just browsing, thank you.
Merci, je regarde seulement.

This is too expensive.
Ca, c'est trop cher.

I need to buy some groceries.
Je dois faire des courses.

We need to buy some bread.
Il faut acheter du pain.

She bought oil and pastry
Elle a acheté d'huile et des pates.

I need some glue.
Il me faut la colle.

Don't forget to buy bonbons for us!
N'oublie pas de nous acheter des bonbons!

We will also take ham.
On prendra aussi du jambon.

What cheese do you want to buy?
Quel fromage veux-tu acheter?

I don't know. I will go and see the cheese department.
Je ne sais pas. J'irai voir le rayon des fromages.

Who will do the shopping the next day?
Qui fera les courses le lendemain?

We will take two bottles of beer.
Nous prenons deux bouteilles de bière.

Give me one liter of oil.
Donnez-moi un litre d'huile.

I didn't buy anything.
Je n'ai rien acheté.

I saw a lot of beautiful things.
J'ai vu beaucoup de belles choses.

I wanted to buy black some trousers for my husband.
Pour mon mari j'ai voulu acheter un pantalon noir.

This dress is very beautiful, but pretty much expensive.
Cette robe est très jolie, mais assez chère.

She goes shopping very often.
Elle fait souvent les magasins.

He is buying shoes.
Il achète des chaussures.

Can I order this online?
Puis-je commander cela sur l'Internet?

At what time does the store open?
À quelle heure le magasin ouvre-t-il ?

Where is the department with women's clothes?
Où est le rayon des vêtements femmes?

Travel

Voyage {wahyazh}

Phrases

taxi

taxi *{taxee}*

taxi stand
station de taxis *{stasyohn dę taxee}*

train

train *{trehn}*

railway station
gare

boat
bateau *{bahtoh}*

port
port *{pohr}*

ship
navire *{naveer}*

ferry

ferry-boat *{fehreebot}*

bus

autobus *{otobuus}*

bus station
arrêt de bus *{areht de buus}*

airport
aéroport *{ehropohr}*

airplane
avion *{avyohn}*

metro
métro *{metroh}*

museum

musée *{muuzay}*

theatre
théâtre *{tehatr}*

cinema

cinéma *{sinehmah}*

casino

casino *{kaseenoh}*

nightlife

vie nocturne *{vee noktuurn}*

park

parc *{park}*

bridge

pont *{pohn}*

Feudal castle

château *{shatoh}*

waterfall

cascade {kaskahd}

garden

jardin *{zhardehn}*

church

église *{egleez}*

monastery

monastère *{monahstehr}*

town hall

mairie *{mehree}*

swimming pool

piscine *{peeseen}*

lake

lac *{lak}*

sports ground

aire de jeu *{ehr dẹ zhuu}*

beach

plage *{plazh}*

valley
vallée *{valay}*

dam

barrage {barahzh}

ravine

ravine *{rahveen}*

town gate

porte de la ville *{port dẹ lah veey}*

forest

foret *{foreh}*

currency

monnaie *{moneh}*

car rental
location voiture *{lokasyohn watuur}*

excursion

excursion *{ekskuursyohn}*

sightseeing
visite guidée *{veezeet geeday}*

walking tour
visite à pied *{veezeet apyeh}*

ski

ski *{skee}*

nature
nature *{natuur}*

mountains

montagnes *{mohntany}*

painting

peinture *{pahntuur}*

camping

camping *{kahnpeehn}*

hut

hutte *{uut}*

customs

douane *{dwahn}*

embassy

ambassade *{ahnbasahd}*

tourist guide
guide touristique *{geed tooreesteek}*

map
carte *{kart}*

Traveling Phrases

Expressions en voyage

Where is the train station?
Ou est la gare?

Which bus goes to the downtown?
Quel bus va dans le centre-ville?

Which line should I take?
Quelle ligne dois-je prendre?

How much does the ticket cost?
Combien coute un billet?

Where do I change trains?
Ou dois-je changer de train?

How many stations are there till downtown?
Combien y a t'il d'arrêtes jusqu'au centre-ville?

You have to get off here
Vous devez descendre ici.

When does the last bus leave?
Quand part le dernier bus?

Do you have a ticket?
Avez-vous un billet?

He travels by boat.
Il va en bateau.

Is it dangerous here?
Est-ce que c'est dangereux ici?

I am lost
Je suis perdu.

We took a wrong way.
Nous nous sommes trompes de chemin.

We have to go back
Nous devons faire demi-tour.

Is there a parking here?
Y a t il un parking ici?

Do you ski?
Faites vous du ski?

Are you going up with a ski-elevator?
Est ce que tu montes avec le téléski?

Where is the tourist office?
Ou est le syndicat d'initiative?

Do you have a city-map for me?
Pourriez-vous me procurer un plan de la ville?

Where is the old town?
Ou est la vieille ville?

Where is the cathedral?
Ou est la cathédrale?

Museum is on the other side.
Le musée se trouve de l'autre côté.

Is the market opened on Sundays?
Est ce que le marché est ouvert le dimanche?

Is taking photos allowed?
Peut-on photographier?

How much does the entrance cost?
Combien coûte l'entrée?

Is there a discount for groups?
Y a t il une réduction pour les groups?

What is this building?
Quel est ce bâtiment?

How old is this bridge?
De quand date ce pont?

Is there any tickets left for the theatre?
Est ce qu'il y a encore des places pour le théâtre?

Can you recommend me something?
Pouvez-vous me recommander quelque chose?

Jobs and Professions

Emplois et les professions {emplwa eh leh profesyohn}

Phrases

doctor
médecin *{medsahn}*

pharmacist
pharmacien *{farmasyahn}*

dentist
dentiste *{dahnteest}*

surgeon
chirurgien *{sheeruurzhyahn}*

journalist
journaliste *{zhoornaleest}*

vendor
vendeur *{vahndewr}*

engineer
ingénieur *{ahnzhenyewr}*

accountant
comptable *{kohntabl}*

lawyer
avocat *{avohkah}*

architect
architecte *{arsheetekt}*

astronaut
astronaute *{astronot}*

postman
facteur *{faktewr}*

veterinarian
vétérinaire *{vetereenehr}*

pilot
pilote *{peelot}*

chef
chef *{shef}*

artist
artiste *{arteest}*

dancer
danseur *{dahnsewr}*

fashion designer
modéliste *{modeleest}*

farmer
agriculteur *{agrikooltewr}*

police officer
policier *{poleesyeh}*

teacher
enseignant *{ahnsenyahn}*

writer
écrivain *{ekreevahn}*

politician
politicien *{poleeteesyahn}*

actor
acteur *{aktewr}*

nurse
infirmier *{ehnfirmyay}*

publisher
éditeur *{editewr}*

editor
rédacteur *{redaktewr}*

carpenter
charpentier *{sharpahntyeh}*

judge

juge *{zhuuzh}*

librarian

bibliothécaire *{beebleeothekehr}*

chemist
chimiste *{sheemeest}*

economist
économiste *{ekonomeest}*

musician
musicien *{muuzeesyehn}*

physicist
physicien *{feezeesyahn}*

car mechanic
mécanicien *{mekaneesyahn}*

laboratory technician
technicien de laboratoire {tekneesyahn d¢ laboratwar}

interior designer
architecte d'intérieur *{arsheetekt dahnteryewr}*

real estate agent
agent immobilier *{azhahn eemobeelyay}*

social worker
assistant social *{aseestahn sosyal}*

web developer
web développeur *{veb devlopewr}*

photographer
photographe *{fotograhf}*

surveyor
géomètre *{zheohmetr}*

system analyst
analyste organique *{analeest organeek}*

firefighter
pompier *{pohnpyeh}*

diver
plongeur *{plahnzhewr}*

driver
chauffeur *{shofewr}*

swimmer
nageur {nazhewr}

electrician
électricien *{elektreesyahn}*

professor
professeur *{profesewr}*

psychologist
psychologue *{pseekolog}*

Profession-related phrases

Expressions liés au travail

What is your profession?
Que faites vous dans la vie?

My husband is a doctor.
Mon mari est le médecin.

I work part-time as a nurse
Je travaille comme infirmière à mi-temps.

I will retire soon.
Je pars bientôt à la retraite.

Our taxes are very high.
Nos impôts sont très élèves.

Health insurance is expensive.
L'assurance maladie est chère.

What would you like to become?
Que veux-tu faire plus tard?

I want to become an engineer.
Je voudrais devenir ingénieur.

I want to study at the university.
Je veux étudier à l'université.

I do not make a lot of money.
Je ne gagne pas beaucoup.

I am looking for a job.
Je cherche du travail.

Please, call the police!
Appelez la police, s'il vous plait!

I want to go to the dentist.
Je veux aller chez le dentiste.

I work full time as a photographer.
Je travaille à plein temps comme un photographier.

I work as a librarian in a local library.
Je travaille comme bibliothécaire dans une bibliothèque locale.

I practice swimming.
Je pratique la natation.

I go to the psychiatrist.
Je vais chez le psychiatre.

I need to take my car to the car mechanic.
Il faut que je prenne ma voiture chez un mécanicien

She is a famous writer.
Elle est un écrivain célèbre.

I love that actor.
J'aime bien cet acteur.

Food

La Nourriture {lah nooreetuur}

Phrases

bread

pain *{pahn}*

butter
beurre *{bewr}*

cheese

fromage *{frohmazh}*

yogurt

yaourt *{yaoort}*

milk
lait *{leh}*

egg

œuf *{ewf}*

sugar

sucre *{suukr}*

flour

farine *{fareen}*

bean
haricot *{areekoh}*

meat

viande *{vyahnd}*

bacon
bacon *{behkehn}*

chicken

poulet *{pooleh}*

beef

bœuf *{bewf}*

pork

porc *{pohr}*

ham

jambon *{zhahnbohn}*

fruit

fruit *{frwee}*

strawberry

fraise *{frehz}*

apple

pomme *{pohm}*

watermelon
melon *{mélohn}*

banana

banane *{banan}*

grape

raisin *{rehzahn}*

oranges

orange *{orahnzh}*

lemon

citron *{seetrohn}*

pear

poire *{pwar}*

peach
pêche *{pehsh}*

berry

baie *{beh}*

cherry

cerise *{sẹreez}*

plum

prune *{pruun}*

vegetable

légume *{leguum}*

broccoli

brocoli *{brokolee}*

tomato

tomate *{tomaht}*

potato

pomme de terre *{pom dẹ tehr}*

carrot

carotte *{kahrot}*

mushroom

champignon *{shahnpeenyohn}*

onion

oignon *{onyohn}*

lettuce

laitue *{letuu}*

corn

maïs *{mahees}*

cabbage

chou *{shoo}*

garlic
ail *{ahy}*

cream
crème *{krehm}*

oil
huile *{weel}*

honey

miel *{myehl}*

ice cream
glaçon *{glasohn}*

cake

gâteau *{gatoh}*

cookie

biscuit *{biskwee}*

nut
noix *{nwa}*

fish

poisson *{pwasohn}*

pancake

crêpe *{krehp}*

rice

riz *{ree}*

salt
sel *{sel}*

Food-related Phrases

Expressions liées à la nourriture

I have one apple.
J'ai une pomme.

I have one orange and one grape.
J'ai une orange et un raisin.

I bought potato and broccoli.
J'ai acheté de la pomme de terre et du brocoli.

I am making a fruit salad.
Je fais une salade de fruits.

I am eating a toast.
Je mange un toast.

I took some bread with butter.
Je pris le pain avec du beurre.

I am eating a sandwich with ham and tomato.
Je mange un sandwich avec du jambon et des tomates.

We need cabbage and pork.

Nous avons besoin de chou et de porc.

We need broccoli and flour for the soup.

Nous avons besoin de brocoli et de la farine pour la soupe.

Do you want some cheese?

Voulez vous du fromage ?

You are as red as a tomato.
Tu es rouge comme une tomate.

The first meal of the day is a breakfast.
Le premier repas de la journée c'est le petit déjeuner.

My breakfast consists of bread, butter and marmalade.

Mon petit déjeuner est composé du pain, beurre et de la confiture.

Cheese is a dairy product.

Le fromage est un produit laitier.

Would you like to eat something?
Voulez-vous manger quelque chose ?

I would like some cake with whipped cream.
Je voudrais un gâteau avec de la crème chantilly.

Would you like some toast with sausage and cheese?

Voulez-vous des toasts avec de la saucisse et du fromage?

I like corn very much.

J'aime bien le maïs.

What kind of vegetables do you have?

Qu'est ce que vous aves comme légumes?

Do you have mushrooms?
Avez-vous des champignons ?

Do you also like paprika?

Aimez-vous aussi le poivron?

I don't like garlic.

Je n'aime pas l'ail.

I would like to eat something without meat.
Je voudrais manger quelque chose sans viande.

Do you like strawberries with cream?
Aimez-vous les fraises avec de la crème?

Do you want some salt?
Voulez-vous du sel?

You need to buy meat and vegetables.
Tu dois acheter de la viande et des légumes.

Do you know how to make pancakes?
Savez-vous comment faire des crêpes?

Do you like your breakfast sweet or salty?

Aimez-vous votre petit-déjeuner sucré ou salé?

I am making rice and fish.
Je fais du poisson avec du riz.

I need some more sugar.
J'ai besoin un peu plus de sucre.

Drinks

Boissons *{bwasohn}*

Phrases

water

eau *{oh}*

mineral water

eau minérale *{oh minerahl}*

tea

thé *{teh}*

coffee

café *{kafeh}*

white wine

vin blanc *{vahn blahn}*

red wine

vin rouge *{vahn roozh}*

alcohol

alcool *{alkohl}*

juice

jus *{zhuu}*

champagne

champagne *{shahnpany}*

cognac

cognac *{kohnyak}*

cocktail

cocktail *{koktehl}*

beer

bière *{byehr}*

whiskey

whisky *{weeskee}*

rum
rhum *{rhoom}*

milk
lait *{lay}*

cacao
cacao *{kakao}*

apple juice
jus de pomme *{zhuu de pohm}*

strawberry juice
jus de fraises *{zhuu de frehz}*

lemonade
limonade *{leemonad}*

orange juice
jus d'orange *{zhuu dorahnzh}*

Drinks-related Phrases

EXPRESSIONS LIÉES aux BOISSONS

I drink tea.
Je bois du thé.

Dou you want coffee?
Voulez-vous du café?

She drinks mineral water.

Elle boive de l'eau minérale.

Do you want some sugar with your tea?

Veux-tu un peu de sucre avec ton thé?

Do you want some ice?
Voulez-vous du glaçon?

People drink champaign.
Les gents boivent du champagne.

Do you drink alcohol?

Bois-tu de l'alcool?

Do you want some whiskey?

Veux-tu en peu de whisky?

My son likes milk.
Mon fils aime le lait.

My wife prefers orange juice.
Ma femme préfère jus d'orange.

Hotels and Accommodation

Hôtels et Hébergement

Phrases

hotel
hôtel *{otel}*

room
chambre *{shahnbr}*

double-room
chambre double *{shahnbr doobl}*

bathroom
salle de bains *{sahl dé bahn}*

bed
lit *{lee}*

breakfast
petit déjeuner *{pétee dehzhewneh}*

lunch
déjeuner *{dehzhewneh}*

dinner

dîner *{deeneh}*

night
nuit *{nwee}*

to book

réserver *{rezehrveh}*

cancel
annuler *{anuleh}*

check-in
arrivée *{ahreevay}*

check-out
départ *{depahr}*

date
date *{dat}*

parking
parking *{pahrkeen}*

key
clé *{kleh}*

heating
chauffage *{shohfazh}*

terrace
terrasse *{tehras}*

air-condition
climatisation *{kleemateezasyohn}*

luggage
bagage *{bagazh}*

Hotel-related Phrases

Expressions liées aux Hôtels

Hello, do you have any free rooms?
Bonjour, avez-vous des chambres libres ?

I booked one room yesterday.
Hier, j'ai réservé une chambre.

I want a single room.
Je voudrais une chambre simple.

Do you want a double room?
Voulez-vous une chambre double ?

Can I see the room please?
Puis-je voir la chambre, s'il vous plait ?

How much does one night cost here?
Combien coûte la nuit ici ?

Is the bathroom equipped with a bathtub or shower?
Est ce que la salle de bain équipée d'une douche ou d'une baignoire?

Do all rooms have bathrooms?
Est ce que toutes les chambres ont des salles de bains ?

Are the pets allowed in this hotel?
Les animaux sont-ils admis dans cet hôtel ?

Do you have an internet service?
Avez-vous un service Internet ?

Is there a parking lot here?

Y a-t-il un parking ici ?

Very nice, I will take the room.

Très bon, je prends la chambre.

At what time is the breakfast?

A quelle heure est le petit déjeuner servi ?

The room is too small and too noisy!
La chambre est trop petite et trop bruyante !

The room doesn't have a terrace.

La chambre n'a pas de terrasse.

Can I use the fax machine?
Puis-je utiliser le fax ?

This is my luggage.
Ceci est mon bagage.

Where is the elevator?
Où est l'ascenseur ?

Shower isn't working.
Douche ne fonctionne pas.

A child in the room next to ours does not stop yelling.
Un enfant dans la chambre à côté du nôtre n'arrête pas de crier.

Can you give us another room, please?
Pouvez-vous nous donner une autre chambre, s'il vous plaît ?

Sports

Sport {spohr}

Phrases

swimming
natation *{natasyohn}*

running
course *{koors}*

jumping

sauter *{soteh}*

orienteering
course d'orientation *{koors doryahntasyohn}*

bowling

boules *{bool}*

dancing

danse *{dahns}*

tennis

tennis *{tenees}*

martial arts
arts martiaux *{ar marsyoh}*

skiing

ski *{skee}*

soccer

football *{footbohl}*

badminton

badminton *{badmeentohn}*

volleyball
volley-ball *{vohlebohl}*

golf

golf *{golf}*

billiard
billard *{beeyahr}*

skating
patinage *{pateenazh}*

basketball

basket *{baskeht}*

hockey
hockey *{okeh}*

athletics
athlétisme *{atleteesm}*

gymnastic
gymnastique *{zheemnasteek}*

rugby
rugby *{roogbee}*

auto racing
compétition automobile *{kohnpeteesyohn otomobeel}*

chess
échecs *{eshek}*

handball
handball *{ahndbal}*

rowing

aviron *{aveerohn}*

archery
tir à l'arc *{teer alark}*

baseball
base-ball *{behzbohl}*

snowboarding
surf des neiges *{sewrf de nehzh}*

boxing

boxe *{boks}*

karate

karaté *{karahteh}*

judo

judo *{zhuudo}*

Sports-related phrases

Expressions liées aux Sport

Do you practice some sport?
Est-ce que tu pratiques un sport ?

I am playing basketball.
Je joue au basket.

I watched one football game on TV.

j'ai regardé un match de football à la télé.

I would like to practice rowing.
Je voudrais pratiquer l'aviron.

My sister is a karate champion.
Ma sœur est une championne de karaté.

I don't know how to swim.
Je ne sais pas nager.

Every winter I practice winter sports.
Chaque hiver, je pratique les sports d'hiver.

My brother thought me to ride a bicycle.
Mon frère m'a appris à faire du vélo.

I like to watch gymnastics competitions.
J'aime bien regarder les concours de gymnastique.

My favorite sport is archery.
Mon sport préféré est tir à l'arc.

Weather

Temps {tahn}

Phrases

sun
soleil *{soley}*

moon
lune *{luun}*

wind

vent *{vahn}*

windy
venteux *{vahntew}*

rain

pluie *{plwee}*

cloud

nuage *{nwazh}*

cloudy
nuageux *{nwazhew}*

warm
chaud *{sho}*

cold

froid *{frwa}*

umbrella

parapluie *{paraplwee}*

sky

ciel *{sjehl}*

forecast

prévisions météo *{preveezyohn meteoh}*

sunshine
ensoleillement *{ahnsoleymahn}*

snow

neige *{nezh}*

ice
glace *{glas}*

slippery

glissant *{gleesahn}*

fog

brouillard *{brooyahr}*

temperature

temperature *{tahnperatuur}*

climate

climat *{kleema}*

altitude

altitude *{alteetuud}*

Weather-related Phrases

Expressions liées au temps

Sun is shining in summer.
Le soleil brille en été.

Winter is often very cold.
L'hiver est souvent très froid.

In winter, it's either raining or snowing.
En hiver, il pleut ou il neige.

It is very cold outside.

Il fait très froid dehors.

Everything is covered with snow.
Tout est couvert de neige.

What is the weather like today?

Comment est le temps aujourd'hui ?

There is fog and it's windy.

Il y a du brouillard et c'est venteux.

Today is sunny and it's warmer.

Aujourd'hui c'est ensoleillé et il fait plus chaud.

Did you bring your umbrella?

As-tu apporté ton parapluie ?

What is the forecast for tomorrow?
Quelles sont les prévisions pour demain ?

Places

Endroits {ahndrwa}

Phrases

bar
pub *{pewb}*

cemetery

cimetière *{seemtyehr}*

disco
discothèque *{diskotehk}*

fast food
restaurant rapide *{restorahn rapeed}*

coffee shop
cafétéria *{kafetehrya}*

monument

monument *{mohnyuumahn}*

zoo

zoo *{zo}*

art gallery
galerie d'art *{galree dahr}*

history museum
musée historique *{muuzeh eestoreek}*

botanical garden
jardin botanique *{zhardahn botaneek}*

carnival
carnaval *{karnaval}*

theme park
parc d'attractions *{park datraksyohn}*

landmark
site d'intérêt *{sit dahntereh}*

adventure

aventure *{avahntuur}*

campus
campus *{kahnpuus}*

boutique
boutique *{booteek}*

wildlife
faune *{fon}*

library

bibliothèque *{beebleeyothek}*

battlefield
champ de bataille *{shahn dę batahy}*

triumphal arch
arc de triomphe *{ark dę treeyohnf}*

river bank

rive *{reev}*

bank

banque *{bahnk}*

square

place *{plas}*

avenue

avenue *{avęnuu}*

inn
auberge *{oberzh}*

prison

prison *{preezohn}*

skyscraper
gratte-ciel *{gratsyehl}*

aquarium
aquarium *{akwareeohm}*

column

colonne *{kolon}*

gravestone
pierre tombale *{pyehr tohnbahl}*

monolith
monolithe *{monoleet}*

obelisk

obélisque *{obeleesk}*

temple

temple *{tahnpl}*

mausoleum
mausolée *{mozoleh}*

island

île *{eel}*

castle

château *{shatoh}*

bookstore

librairie *{leebreree}*

court

cour *{koor}*

craft market
marché artisanal *{marsheh arteezanal}*

fire station
caserne de pompiers *{kazehrn de pohnpye}*

laundromat
laverie *{lavree}*

gallery

galerie *{galree}*

school

école *{ekohl}*

traffic

circulation *{seerkuulasyohn}*

police station

commissariat de police *{komeesarya de polees}*

gym

salle de sport *{sal de spor}*

gas station

station-service *{stasyohn servees}*

department store

grand magasin *{grohn magazahn}*

hospital

hôpital *{opeetal}*

banc

banc *{bahn}*

Places-related Phrases

Expressions liées aux endroits

Is this museum open on Wednesdays?

Ce musée, ouvre t'il le mercredi ?

I have to go to the bank.

Je dois allez à la banque.

Yesterday I was shopping in the department store.

Hier, je faisais des courses dans le grand magasin.

Do you want to take a walk through this botanical garden?
Veux-tu se promener dans ce jardin botanique ?

I would like to go to the zoo.

J'aimerais aller au zoo.

Is there a gas station nearby?
Y a-t-il une station service à proximité ?

Could you please tell me how to find the nearest hospital?
Pourriez-vous me dire comment trouver l'hôpital le plus proche ?

My sister works in this bookstore.
Ma sœur travaille dans cette librairie.

Let's have a drink in this pub!

Allons boire un verre dans ce pub !

This city has a beautiful cathedral.
Cette ville a une belle cathédrale.

She is frequently going to the gym.
Elle va souvent à la salle de sport.

How can we reach the castle?
Comment peut-on accéder au château ?

Where is the police station?
Où est le commissariat ?

Do you want to go to the craft market?
Voulez-vous aller au marché artisanal ?

There is a famous mausoleum on this cemetery.
Il ya un mausolée célèbre dans ce cimetière.

This building served as a prison in the middle ages.
Ce bâtiment a servi de prison au Moyen-âge.

This triumphal arc was built to celebrate a great victory.

Cet arc de triomphe été construit pour célébrer une grande victoire.

There are no skyscrapers in this city?
Il n'y a pas des gratte-ciel dans cette ville ?

Do you go to school here?
Vous aller à l'école ici ?

I love to go to the theme park.
J'aime aller au parc d'attractions.

Emotions

Émotions {emosyohn}

Phrases

happy
heureux *{ewrew}*

sad

triste *{treest}*

cry
pleurer *{plewreh}*

smile
sourire *{sooreer}*

feel
sentir *{sahnteer}*

envy

envier *{ahnvee}*

sadness
tristesse *{treestes}*

careful
prudent *{pruudahn}*

reserved
réservé *{rehzervay}*

mood

humeur *{uumewr}*

bored
ennuyé *{ahnyeeyay}*

curious
curieux *{kooryew}*

eager

impatient *{ahnpasyahn}*

hungry
avoir faim *{avwar fahn}*

thirsty
assoiffée *{aswafe}*

pleased

content *{kohntahn}*

unhappy
malheureux *{mahlewrew}*

scared

avoir peur *{avwar pewr}*

fearless

courageux *{koorazhew}*

love
amour *{amoor}*

hate

haine *{ehn}*

jealousy

jalousie *{zhaloozee}*

tense

tendu *{tahnduu}*

surprised

étonné *{etohnay}*

angry

fâché *{fashay}*

indifference
indifférence *{ahndeeferahns}*

proud

fier *{fyehr}*

confused
confus *{kohnfuu}*

melancholic
mélancolique *{melahnkoleek}*

ashamed
avoir honte *{avwar ohnt}*

Emotions-related phrases

Expressions liées aux emotions

I am very happy.

Je suis très heureux.

Are you feeling sad?
Tu te sens triste ?

Why are you crying?

Pourquoi pleurs-tu ?

She is jealous of you.
Elle est jalouse de toi.

I am hungry.

J'ai faim.

He is proud of you.

Il est fier de toi.

Don't be angry.

Ne te fâche pas.

You have a beautiful smile.

Tu as un beau sourire.

She is impatient to go.
Elle est impatiente d'aller.

Are you thirsty?
Avez-vous soif ?

He is a reserved person.
Il est une personne réservée.

I am not in the mood.
Je n'ai pas d'envie.

Are you bored?
Vous ennuyez-vous ?

He is curious.
Il est curieux.

Your arrogance is unbelievable.
Votre arrogance est incroyable.

I am surprised she decided to come.
Je suis surpris qu'elle ait décidé de venir.

She is constantly melancholic.
Elle est toujours mélancolique.

I am feeling tense around him.
Je me sens tendue autour de lui.

His hatred is repulsive.
Sa haine est répugnante.

Be careful when you go there.
Soyez prudent quand vous allez là-bas.

50 Survival Phrases

Good day.
Bonjour.

Good evening.
Bonsoir.

Good bye.
Au revoir.

Thank you very much.
Merci beaucoup.

You are welcome.
De rien.

Please, help me!
S'il vous plaît, aider moi !

How are you?
Comment allez-vous ?

I am very well, thank you.
Je vais très bien, merci.

What is your name?

Comment tu t'appelle ?

My name is...
Je m'appelle...

Nice to meet you.
Enchanté.

How do you say... in French?
Comment dites-vous ... en français ?

How old are you?
Quel âge as-tu ?

I don't understand.
Je ne comprends pas.

Could you please say it one more time more slowly?
Pourriez-vous répéter plus lentement, s'il vous plaît ?

Do you understand?
Est-ce que tu comprends ?

Do you speak English?
Parlez-vous anglais ?

Do you speak French?
Parles-tu français ?

I speak German.
Je parle allemand.

I don't speak Japanese.
Je ne parle pas japonais.

Could you please help me?
Pourriez-vous m'aider s'il vous plaît ?

Of course, what do you need?
Bien sûr, de quoi avez-vous besoin ?

Don't worry, I will help you.
Ne vous inquiétez pas, je vais vous aider.

Good luck.
Bonne chance.

Congratulations.
Félicitations.

I don't know.
Je ne sais pas.

Where are you from?
Tu viens d'où ?

I live in Washington.
J'habite à Washington.

He is from New York.
Il vient de New York.

How can I help you?
Comment puis-je vous aider ?

Can you please show me where is bus station?
Pouvez-vous me montrer où se trouve la station de bus ?

Can you please show me on the map?
Pouvez-vous me montrer sur la carte, s'il vous plaît ?

I need a drink.
J'ai besoin d'une boisson.

I am hungry.
J'ai faim.

Where is the hospital?
Où est l'hôpital ?

Where can I change some money into Euros?
Où puis-je changer de l'argent en Euros ?

Can you give me something for my headache?
Pourriez-vous me donner quelque chose pour ma migraine ?

I need something less strong.
J'ai besoin de quelque chose de moins fort.

My family lives in US.
Ma famille habite aux États-Unis.

Hi/Hello
Salut.

Welcome to our city!
Bienvenue dans notre ville !

See you later.
À plus tard.

See you tomorrow.
À demain.

See you soon.
A bientôt.

Where can I buy a map of the city?
Où puis-je acheter une carte de la ville ?

I forgot where that was.
J'ai oublié où c'était.

I love you.
Je t'aime.

I miss you.
Tu me manques.

When will I see you again?
Quand vais-je te revoir ?

Good night
Bon nuit.

I have to go.
Je dois partir.

At the Post Office – Common Phrases

Where is the nearest post office?
Où se trouve le bureau de poste le plus proche ?

Is the nearest post office far from here?
Est-ce que le plus proche bureau de poste loin d'ici ?

Where is the nearest mailbox?
Où se trouve boîte aux lettres la plus proche ?

I want to buy a couple of postal stamps.
Je veux acheter des quelques timbres postaux.

I need stamps for one letter and one postcard.
J'ai besoin de timbres pour une lettre et une carte postale.

How much the shipping for United States costs?
Combien coût l'affranchissement pour l'États Unis ?

How much does the package weigh?
Combien pèse le paquet ?

Can I send the package via air mail?
Puis-je envoyer le paquet par avion ?

How long does it take for mail to arrive?
Combien de temps cela prend pour recevoir son courrier ?

May I use a telephone here?
Puis-je utiliser un téléphone ici ?

Do you know the area code for Switzerland?
Connaissez-vous l'indicatif régional pour la Suisse ?

Please wait one moment, I will take a look.
S'il vous plaît attendez un moment, je vais voir.

Where is the nearest phone box?
Où se trouve la plus proche cabine téléphonique ?

This line is always occupied.
Cette ligne est toujours occupée.

Are there any phone cards for sale?
Y a-t-il des télécartes pour la vente ?

Where can I find a phone book?
Où puis-je trouver un annuaire téléphonique ?

How much does a postcard cost?
Combien coûte une carte postale ?

How many letters have you received?
Combien de lettres avez-vous reçu ?

I love to receive packages!
J'aime recevoir des paquets !

Is it expensive to mail a package to another country?
Est-ce cher d'envoyer un colis dans un autre pays ?

At the Airport – Common Phrases

Hello, I would like to book one ticket for a flight to Paris.
Bonjour, je voudrais réserver un billet d'avion pour Paris.

Are there any direct flights?
Y a t-il des vols directs ?

I prefer a non-smoker seat.
Je préfère une place non-fumeur.

I would like a seat by a window, if possible.
Je voudrais une place près du hublot, si possible.

I would like to confirm my reservation.
Je souhaite confirmer ma réservation.

I would like to cancel my reservation.
Je souhaite annuler ma réservation.

I would like to change my reservation's date.
Je souhaite changer la date de ma réservation.

When is the next flight for Paris?
Quand est le prochain vol pour Paris ?

Can I book two more economy seats?
Puis-je réserver deux autres sièges en classe économique ?

No, we only have one seat left.
Non, nous n'avons plus qu'un seul siège

When do we land?
Quand allons-nous atterrir ?

What will the weather be like during the flight?
Quel temps fera-t-il pendant le vol ?

How many suitcases may I bring along?
Combien de bagages puis-je apporter avec moi ?

What is the weight limit?
Quelle est la limite de poids des bagages ?

Will a lunch be served during the flight?
Est ce que les repas sont servis lors de vol ?

How long will the flight last?
Quelle est la durée de vol ?

How many times will we need to change planes?
Combien de fois nous aurons besoin de changer d'avion ?

Where are the baggage carts?
Où sont les chariots à bagages ?

Can someone please help me with my baggage?
S'il vous plait quelqu'un peut-il m'aider avec mon bagage ?

If I lose my baggage what am I to do?
Si je perds mon bagage que dois-je faire ?

At the Hospital – Common Phrases

Hello, I have an appointment with my doctor today.
Bonjour, j'ai un rendez-vous avec mon médecin aujourd'hui.

My appointment is scheduled for 2 o'clock.
Mon rendez-vous est à deux heures.

What is your name?
Quel-est votre nom ?

Please, take a seat in the waiting room.
Asseyez-vous dans la salle d'attente s'il vous plait.

The doctor will see you right away.
Le docteur va vous voir dans un instant.

Do you have an insurance number?
Avez-vous un numéro d'assurance social ?

Do you have some particular problem?
Est-ce que vous avez un problème particulier ?

Where do you feel pain?
Où est-ce que vous avez mal ?

I have a strong pain in my chest.
J'ai une forte douleur sous ma poitrine.

I suffer from frequent headaches.
Je souffre de maux de têtes fréquents.

Your throat is red and swollen.
Votre gorge est rouge et enflée.

Do you have a temperature?
Avez-vous de la température ?

I had a strong fever yesterday, but I'm feeling better today.
J'ai eu une forte fièvre hier, mais je me sens mieux aujourd'hui.

Please take off your clothes.
Déshabillez-vous, s'il vous plaît.

Please lie down on this couch.
Allongez-vous sur ce canapé s'il vous plaît.

Your blood pressure seems to be fine.
Votre pression artérielle semble être très bien.

I will write a prescription for you.
Je vais rédiger une ordonnance pour vous.

You will need to receive an injection.
Vous aurez besoin de recevoir une injection.

How long do you have these symptoms?
Combien de temps avez-vous ces symptômes ?

You will need to drink these tablets twice a day.
Vous aurez besoin de boire ces comprimés deux fois par jour.

At the Restaurant – Common Phrases

This is one of the best restaurants in the city.
C'est l'un des meilleurs restaurants de la ville.

Is this table free?
Est-ce que cette table est libre ?

I would like to see the menu, please.
J'aimerais voir le menu, s'il vous plaît

What can you recommend to us?
Que pouvez-vous nous recommander ?

I will have a coke, please.
Je vais prendre un coke, s'il vous plaît.

I would like a coffee with warm milk, please.
Je voudrais un café avec au lait chaud, s'il vous plaît.

Do you have an ash-tray?
Avez-vous un cendrier ?

I don't have a fork.
Je n'ai pas une fourchette.

You will need a spoon for that meal.
Vous aurez besoin d'une cuillère pour ce repas.

Would you like a glass of red wine?
Voulez-vous un verre de vin rouge ?

No, I will have a glass of white wine please.
Non, je vais prendre un verre de vin blanc s'il vous plaît.

Do you want to eat sea products?
Voulez-vous manger des produits de la mer ?

Do you like tomato salad with cheese?
Aimez-vous la salade de tomates avec du fromage ?

Would you like some rice with your meal?
Aimeriez-vous un peu de riz en accompagnement ?

Can you bring some more bread, please?
Pourriez-vous nous amener un peu plus de pain, s'il vous plaît ?

I don't like that meal.
Je n'aime pas manger ça.

This meal is cold.
Cette nourriture est froide.

I didn't order soup.
Je n'ai pas commandé la soupe.

It was very tasty.
Il était délicieux.

Give my compliments to the chef.
Donnez mes compliments au chef.

At the School – Common Phrases

I am going to school.
Je vais à l'école.

I am a student.
Je suis étudiant.

My favorite subject is biology.
Ma matière préférée est la biologie.

I have excellent marks.
J'ai d'excellentes notes.

I study very hard for my exams.
J'étudie très dur pour mes examens.

Where is the classroom?
Où est la salle de classe ?

The classroom is down the hall.
La salle de classe est dans le couloir.

What are you reading?
Que lisez-vous ?

I am reading a book for my assignment.
Je lis un livre pour mon devoir.

Are you writing with a pen or pencil?
Écris-tu avec un stylo ou un crayon ?

You have a beautiful pencil case.
Tu as une jolie trousse.

I bought a new notebook with nice covers.
J'ai acheté un nouveau cahier avec la belle couverture.

Do you need a calculator or a ruler?
As-tu besoin d'une calculatrice ou d'une règle ?

My bag is too heavy so I need to bring fewer books.
Mon sac est trop lourd, alors il faut que je prenne moins de livres.

My teacher is very gentle.
Mon maître est très gentil.

I am the best student in our class.
Je suis le meilleur élève de notre classe.

His notebook is on the desk.
Son cahier est sur la table.

This is Mary's felt pen.
C'est le stylo feutre de Mary.

We write with a chalk on the blackboard.
Nous écrire avec une craie sur le tableau.

How many students are there in your class?
Combien d'étudiants y a-t-il dans votre classe ?

Printed in Great Britain
by Amazon

84108669R00086